I CAN BE...

I CAN BE BRAINY

CLEVER SCIENTISTS
WHO CHANGED THE WORLD

BY SHALINI VALLEPUR

Enslow
PUBLISHING

Published in 2021 by Enslow Publishing, LLC
101 W. 23rd Street, Suite 240,
New York, NY 10011

© 2020 Booklife Publishing
This edition is published by arrangement with Booklife Publishing

Cataloging-in-Publication Data

Names: Vallepur, Shalini.
Title: I can be brainy: clever scientists who changed the world / Shalini Vallepur.
Description: New York : Enslow Publishing, 2021. | Series: I can be... | Includes glossary
and index.
Identifiers: ISBN 9781978519596 (pbk.) | ISBN 9781978519619 (library bound) | ISBN
9781978519602 (6 pack)
Subjects: LCSH: Scientists--Biography--Juvenile literature. | Science--History--Juvenile literature.
| Discoveries in science--Juvenile literature.
Classification: LCC Q141.V35 2020 | DDC 509.2'2 B--dc23

Printed in the United States of America

CPSIA compliance information: Batch #BS20ENS: For further information contact Enslow Publishing, New York, New York at 1-800-542-2595

IMAGE CREDITS

All images are courtesy of Shutterstock.com, unless otherwise specified. With thanks to Getty Images, Thinkstock Photo and iStockphoto.
Cover and throughout – asantosg, Forest Foxy, WINS86. 7 – Alevtina_Vyacheslav, Separisa, ShustrikS. 9 – Tartila. 10 – Morphart Creation,
9'63 Creation. 11 – Andrey_Kuzmin, Mitrushova Tatiana. 15 – Ron Dale, Nikola Tesla [Public domain]. 17 – YashkovskiyMD. 19 – Ibooo7. 21
– AlexanderZam, hugolacasse, mhatzapa, KamranSamadov19988991 [CC BY-SA 4.0 (https://creativecommons.org/licenses/by-sa/4.0)],
KLEMIO. 23 – Elina Li, Vectorpocket. 24-25 – Zorech, miniwide, Ruslan Gi. 27 – udaix, Melok. 28 – Airin.dizain.
29 – Andrii Bezvershenko, Shtonado.

CONTENTS

WORDS THAT LOOK LIKE this CAN BE FOUND IN THE GLOSSARY ON PAGE 31.

I CAN BE...
BRAINY

Do you ever wonder where things come from or how they work? How does a smartphone connect to the internet? What makes a car move? Where does our medicine come from? Somebody had to think about these things in order to make them work.

Throughout history, brainy people have been making discoveries and inventions that have changed the world.

A lot of brainy people have faced challenges when working on new projects or ideas. If somebody worked on something that went against the religion of the area, then they could be punished for it. A lot of women were treated differently and didn't have the same chances that men had. Some people were treated differently because of where they came from. Even though these challenges existed, scientists, engineers, and inventors never gave up and kept working hard.

Read on to learn all about the lives of famous scientists and inventors, and you'll see that you can be brainy too!

$E = mc^2$

HYPATIA

Born: Around 355 Died: 415

Hypatia was a Greek woman who lived in Alexandria, Egypt. Her father was a <u>scholar</u> named Theon. He taught Hypatia mathematics and <u>astronomy</u> so she could carry on his work. Theon wanted to make sure that Greek values and teachings were kept alive. These teachings were <u>pagan</u>.

There was a lot of trouble in Alexandria during Hypatia's time. Jews, Christians, and pagans were fighting. Even though it was dangerous to spread pagan teachings, Hypatia kept working. She gave public speeches about the Greek <u>philosophers</u> Plato and Aristotle. She is believed to have invented a new kind of hydrometer, a tool that measures water.

The troubles in Alexandria kept getting worse and soon Hypatia was killed by Christian <u>zealots</u>. It is believed that she was killed for teaching and spreading pagan values.

During her time, Hypatia was known as the world's leading mathematician and astronomer. This was a great achievement as most of the world's scholars at this time were men.

**"TO UNDERSTAND THE THINGS THAT ARE AT OUR DOOR IS THE BEST PREPARATION FOR UNDERSTANDING THOSE THAT LIE BEYOND."
- HYPATIA**

BE LIKE HYPATIA AND INSPIRE PEOPLE TO WORK HARD, EVEN IN THE FACE OF <u>PREJUDICE</u>.

GALILEO GALILEI

Born: 1564 Died: 1642

When Galileo was a young man, he discovered that he had a love for math. Galileo left university to learn about math, philosophy, and astronomy. He studied the philosophers of the past such as Aristotle, and even improved their theories. Galileo began to think in a different way and some people did not like this.

Galileo was amazed when the first spyglass was made in 1609. A spyglass could be used to look at things that were far away. Galileo decided to make his own spyglass. He ended up making a telescope that looked far into the distance. He made huge discoveries using his telescope. He saw <u>craters</u> on the moon and discovered four more moons that were in <u>orbit</u> around Jupiter.

But Galileo's work soon led him to trouble. Galileo supported the idea that the sun was at the center of our solar system, and not Earth. We now know this is true, but at the time, Galileo was accused of <u>heresy</u> and put in prison. When he was let out, he didn't give up on his idea and wrote a book about it.

"MEASURE WHAT CAN BE MEASURED AND MAKE MEASURABLE WHAT CANNOT BE MEASURED."
- GALILEO GALILEI

ISAAC NEWTON

Born: 1642 or 1643 Died: 1727

Isaac Newton had a difficult childhood in Britain. His father died before he was born. When Newton was two years old, he was left in the care of his grandmother. Newton did not do very well at school and was not very good at math. He liked to make things such as clocks and read books on his own.

Newton's mother wanted him to become a farmer, but he wanted to study at a university. He went to the University of Cambridge, where he liked to work and live alone.

Newton made important discoveries in science and spent a lot of time studying <u>gravity</u>. It is said that he saw an apple fall from a tree. He began to wonder how the apple fell straight to the ground.

Newton started off as a lonely child, but his discoveries and inventions in science have gone on to help us understand the world around us.

BE LIKE NEWTON

WATER GRAVITY EXPERIMENT

Newton is famous for his discovery of and work on gravity.
He realized that gravity was an invisible force that keeps everything from flying upward and away. You can be like Newton and investigate gravity!

YOU WILL NEED:

A paper cup

A pencil

A jug of water

A big bucket or
a patch of grass

1. Poke a hole in the paper cup using a sharp pencil. Make sure that the hole is in the side, near the bottom of the cup.

2. Cover the hole with your finger and fill the cup with water from the jug.

3. Stand over a bucket or outside on some grass. Take your finger off the hole.

4. Does water come out of the hole? Write down what happens when you take your finger off the hole.

5. Fill the cup again with your finger over the hole.

6. Stand over a bucket or outside on some grass. Let go of the cup and take your finger off the hole at the same time.

7. Does water come out of the hole? Write down what happens.

Gravity pulls water out of the hole when you take your finger off it. When you let go of the cup, the water and the cup fall down at the same speed, so water doesn't come out of the hole.

NIKOLA TESLA

Born: 1856 Died: 1943

Nikola Tesla became interested in inventing because of his mother. When he was growing up in Croatia, Tesla's mother would invent little things that could be used around the house. Inspired by his mother, Tesla went to college. He soon left to work for Thomas Edison's company.

Tesla worked hard for Edison, who was another famous inventor. Tesla invented a new technology that made transporting electricity easier, but he found it difficult to work with Edison.

Tesla faced many challenges in his career. Even though he was a brainy inventor, there were many times when he couldn't get enough money to fund his work. Tragedy struck when a fire destroyed his laboratory with all his work and machines inside.

Tesla still went on to achieve a lot. He got **patents** for many of his inventions. His work on electricity is still used today, including a special coil that he invented which is used in radio technology.

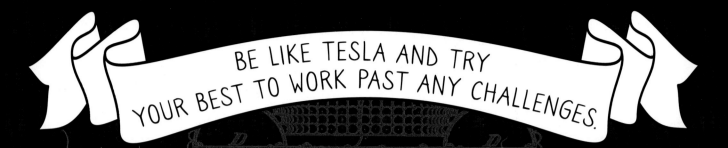

BE LIKE TESLA AND TRY YOUR BEST TO WORK PAST ANY CHALLENGES.

"INVENTION IS THE MOST IMPORTANT PRODUCT OF HUMANKIND'S CREATIVE BRAIN."
- NIKOLA TESLA

MARIE CURIE

Born: 1867 Died: 1934

Marie Curie was born in Poland. When she was born, she was called Maria Salomea Skłodowska, but her family called her Manya. Curie did well at school because her parents were teachers. They encouraged her to read and write.

Life in Poland was tough during Curie's life. Polish people weren't allowed to read or write in Polish, and women were not allowed to go to college. However, Curie wanted to go to college, so she traveled to France and worked until she could afford to go to a university there.

She married Pierre Curie in France. They were both scientists, and they worked together to discover **radiation** and two new **elements**, radium and polonium. Curie named polonium after her home country. Curie was awarded the Nobel Prize for Physics in 1903 and the Nobel Prize for Chemistry in 1911 for these amazing discoveries.

Unfortunately, Pierre Curie was killed in an accident. He left behind Curie and their two daughters. Things were tough, but Curie managed to raise their two daughters alone and carry on working as a scientist. During **World War I**, Curie and her daughter Irene created X-ray trucks to help wounded soldiers.

Curie's work with radiation and X-rays has led to important discoveries, such as X-ray machines that are used in hospitals.

"LIFE IS NOT EASY FOR ANY OF US. BUT WHAT OF THAT? WE MUST HAVE PERSEVERANCE AND ABOVE ALL CONFIDENCE IN OURSELVES."
- MARIE CURIE

BE LIKE CURIE AND CHASE YOUR DREAMS, AND DON'T GIVE UP WHEN THINGS GET TOUGH.

ALBERT EINSTEIN

Born: 1879 Died: 1955

$$E = mc^2$$

Albert Einstein is famous for making some of the most important discoveries in science. He is thought to be one of the cleverest people to have ever lived. He won the Nobel Prize for Physics in 1921 and was a **humanitarian** who spoke out against prejudice.

$$F = \frac{d}{dt}(mv)$$

But Einstein was very different when he was a child growing up in Germany. He wasn't very good at school. Many of his teachers thought that he was not very smart. Einstein didn't like being at school very much. He became interested in math and taught it to himself. His love for math and physics grew, so he went on to study them.

In 1932, when Einstein was 53 years old, he had to leave Germany. Einstein was Jewish, and Germany had become a dangerous place for Jewish people to live. This was because a group of people called the **Nazis**, who hated Jews, were becoming more powerful in Germany. He left Germany to live in the United States.

Einstein made huge discoveries in physics that inspired the world.

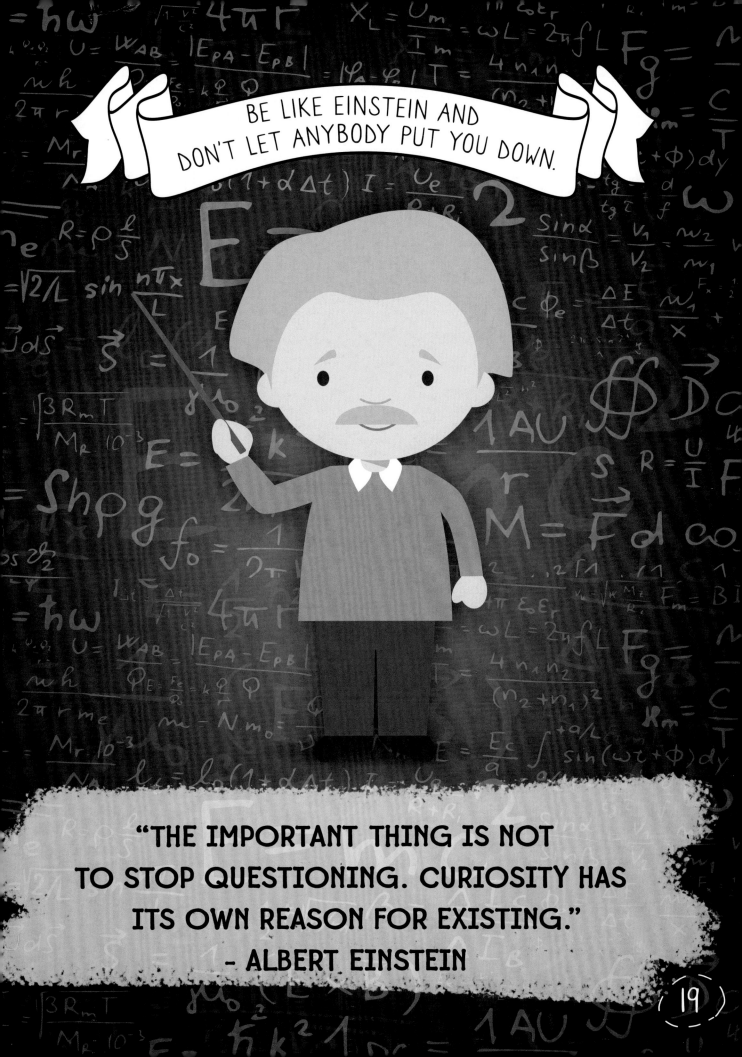

BE LIKE EINSTEIN AND DON'T LET ANYBODY PUT YOU DOWN.

"THE IMPORTANT THING IS NOT TO STOP QUESTIONING. CURIOSITY HAS ITS OWN REASON FOR EXISTING."
- ALBERT EINSTEIN

HEDY LAMARR

Born: 1914 Died: 2000

Hedy Lamarr was born Hedwig Kiesler in Austria. Growing up, Lamarr was inspired by her father to be curious about the world around her. She loved to take her toys apart and figure out how they worked.

As Lamarr grew up, she became interested in acting and started to appear in films. She starred in her first film when she was 16 years old. Her movie career was successful, and she made headlines for her roles. However, she was always interested in how things worked.

In between making films, Lamarr liked to work on her inventions. Lamarr wanted to help people when <u>World War II</u> started. Working with a man called George Antheil, Lamarr invented a system that used <u>radio waves</u> to allow <u>torpedoes</u> to reach their target.

Lamarr is remembered as a famous film star, but she was also a clever inventor. Lamarr's work had an impact on technology that is used today, including GPS, Wi-Fi, and Bluetooth.

BE LIKE LAMARR AND EXPLORE EVERYTHING THAT INTERESTS YOU.

"I MUST MAKE MY OWN DECISIONS, MOLD MY OWN CHARACTER, THINK MY OWN THOUGHTS."
- HEDY LAMARR

KATHERINE JOHNSON

Born: 1918

From a very young age, Katherine Johnson loved numbers. She was born in West Virginia. She did very well at school, but her school did not let black children stay past the eighth grade. So, when she was ten years old, Johnson was sent to a high school away from her hometown.

She finished high school when she was just 14 years old and was one of three black students to be picked to attend college. This was a huge achievement as black students were not allowed to attend many universities at this time.

Johnson joined <u>NASA</u>. It was her job to do calculations without the help of a calculator. She started off working behind the scenes. Johnson refused to be treated differently for being a black American. She pushed herself forward and started to work on big projects. She worked out the numbers for a spacecraft that was carrying astronaut John Glenn around Earth. Later, she helped make calculations for the Apollo mission to the moon.

"I COUNTED EVERYTHING. I COUNTED THE STEPS TO THE ROAD, THE STEPS UP TO CHURCH, THE NUMBER OF DISHES AND SILVERWARE I WASHED...ANYTHING THAT COULD BE COUNTED, I DID."
- KATHERINE JOHNSON

BE LIKE JOHNSON AND LET NOTHING HOLD YOU BACK.

BE LIKE JOHNSON

BUILD A BOTTLE ROCKET

Johnson helped rockets take off into space. You can be like Johnson and launch your own rocket. Will it blast off into the sky?

YOU WILL NEED:

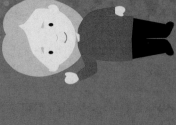

An adult to help

A pencil

Scissors

Tape

Colored paper

An empty plastic milk bottle

1. Ask an adult to cut a big circle out of the paper and then cut the circle into a third.

2. Roll the paper into a cone, and tape it so it holds.

3. Cut small triangles out of another sheet of paper to make fins. Tape them onto the bottom of the cone.

4. Decorate your cone rocket with drawings or your very own space logo.

5. Put the cone rocket on top of the empty plasticbottle.

6. Squeeze the milk bottle, and watch the cone rocket fly!

Now you have your very very own rocket! The cone and the fins will help it soar through the air. What adventures will it go on?

TU YOUYOU

Born: 1930

Tu Youyou grew up in a city in China called Ningbo. When she was 16 years old, she caught a disease called tuberculosis. Even though the disease made her miss school for two years, Tu decided that she wanted to learn how to keep herself and other people healthy, so she studied **pharmacology**.

The Chinese government was looking for medicine to treat a disease called malaria. Malaria is a disease that affects people all over the world. Tu was interested in Chinese medicine and how plants can be used for medicine. She realized that a cure for malaria could be found in the plants that have been used in Chinese medicine for over 2,000 years.

Tu discovered a medicine that helps treat malaria in a plant called sweet wormwood. Although she found the medicine, she was not able to **publish** the work that was done until many years after. This was because of certain rules set by the government.

Tu's discovery has saved the lives of millions of people around the world. She shares a Nobel Prize for Medicine for her discovery.

BE LIKE YOUYOU AND THINK OUTSIDE THE BOX TO FIND NEW WAYS TO SOLVE PROBLEMS.

"IT IS MY DREAM THAT CHINESE MEDICINE WILL HELP US CONQUER LIFE-THREATENING DISEASES WORLDWIDE."
- TU YOUYOU

STEPHEN HAWKING

Born: 1942 Died: 2018

Stephen Hawking was born in Oxford, England. When he
was a young boy, he would look up at the night sky and all
the stars. Hawking loved to be outside and make things such as
computers. He studied physics and **cosmology** so that he could
learn about space, stars, and the universe.

When Hawking was 21, he was diagnosed with ALS. ALS is
a condition that makes muscles in the body get weaker and weaker
until they can't be used. Hawking was told that he had two years
left to live.

This made Hawking work harder than ever. He finished his studies
at school and went on to do important research on **black holes**.
Over time, Hawking became unable to talk and could only move
his fingers. He had a special computer on his wheelchair
that he used to talk.

Hawking's work was very complicated, so he wrote books that
made his work easy to understand for people without his scientific
background. Anybody could read and learn about space.

Hawking's research led him to win lots of awards and medals
and inspire people all over the world.

"HOWEVER DIFFICULT LIFE MAY SEEM, THERE IS ALWAYS SOMETHING YOU CAN DO AND SUCCEED AT. IT MATTERS THAT YOU DON'T JUST GIVE UP."
- STEPHEN HAWKING

BE LIKE HAWKING AND NEVER EVER GIVE UP.

MORE BRAINY PEOPLE

There are many more scientists and inventors
to inspire you!

CHARLES DARWIN

Born: 1809 Died: 1882

Darwin's theory of evolution changed
scientific thought. He suggested that
humans and animals shared **ancestors**.
A lot of people disagreed with his theory at
first, but it helped to change science and
inspired many scientists across the world.

ADA LOVELACE

Born: 1815 Died: 1852

Lovelace became the first computer
programmer in history. Early computers
were huge machines that could only do
calculations. Lovelace wanted to improve
computers so they could do lots more. Her
work on computers inspires people today.

ALICE BALL

Born: 1892 Died: 1916

Ball was the first woman and first
black American to earn a master's
degree from the University of Hawaii. She
worked as a chemist and discovered a
treatment that helped people suffering
from Hansen's disease (also known as
leprosy), changing their lives and how
we treat the disease.

ALAN TURING

Born: 1912 Died: 1954

During World War II, mathematician and
computer scientist Turing worked to break
enemy codes. His success at breaking
codes and his "Turing test" helped the war
efforts, and he was called the "father of the
computer." Turing was gay, which was illegal
at that time. After the war, he was arrested
for being gay. He died a few years later.

GLOSSARY

ancestors   people from whom one is descended, for example great-grandparents

astronomy   the study of the universe and objects in space

black holes   bodies in space that have an extremely strong gravitational pull

cosmology   the study of nature and the origins of the universe

craters   bowl-shaped, hollow areas left on a surface

elements   substances that cannot be broken down into other substances

gravity   the force that pulls things toward large objects in space, such as planets or suns

heresy   an opinion or belief that goes against what is widely believed

humanitarian   somebody who wants to improve the quality of life for people everywhere

NASA   National Aeronautics and Space Administration of the United States

Nazis   members of a political party that controlled Germany from 1933 to 1945 and fought in World War II

orbit   a path that an object makes around bigger objects in space

pagan   beliefs or religions that worship many gods

patents   documents, usually given by a government, that allow somebody to make, use, or sell an invention

pharmacology   the science of making and giving out medicines

philosophers   people who study the nature of knowledge, reality, and existence

prejudice   an opinion, judgment, or belief that is made without taking the facts into account

publish   to print something that is sold or given out to the public

radiation   energy traveling in waves or particles, given off by some materials or devices, which can be harmful in large doses

radio waves   types of electromagnetic waves that can travel huge distances and still be understood

scholar   somebody who studies and researches a topic

torpedoes   explosive missiles that are launched under water to use against ships

World War I   a war fought between 1914 and 1918

World War II   a war fought between 1939 and 1945

zealots   people who are fanatical about a religion or other ideals

INDEX